COACHING
KIDS
TO
PLAY
BASEBALL
AND
SOFTBALL

by
KURT ASCHERMANN
and
GERARD P. O'SHEA

Photographs by Susan C. Daboll

A FIRESIDE BOOK
Published by Simon & Schuster, Inc.
New York

I dedicate this book with love to my father, Ernie, who not only taught me how to play the game, and suffered with my strikeouts and exulted in my homers, but also taught me that winning is important . . . but not that important.

K.A.

To my son Mitchell O'Shea for his contributions at our Coach-the-Coach Clinics, and to all the children who learn to enjoy playing ball as much as their parents.

G.P.O.

Copyright © 1985 by Gerard P. O'Shea Associates and Kurt Aschermann

A Fireside Book

Published by Simon & Schuster, Inc.
Simon & Schuster Building
Rockefeller Center
1230 Avenue of the Americas
New York, New York 10020

FIRESIDE and colophon are registered trademarks of Simon & Schuster, Inc.

Designed by Stanley S. Drate/Folio Graphics Co., Inc.

Manufactured in the United States of America

10 9 8 7 6 5

Library of Congress Cataloging in Publication Data

Aschermann, Kurt.
   Coaching kids to play baseball and softball.

   1. Baseball for children—Coaching. 2. Softball for children—Coaching. I. O'Shea, Gerard P. II. Title.
GV875.5.A84   1985   796.357′024055   84-27752

ISBN: 0-671-55536-7

CONTENTS

Foreword   9

By Jeff Torborg, New York Yankees coach

Preface   11

1 **Building the Team, Child by Child**   13

Whether the team you coach does or does
not enjoy the season; whether or not they
increase their love of baseball or softball
depends on you, Coach, on your
understanding of your players and your
behavior toward your team.

2 **Planning a Meaningful Practice**   18

You can build self-esteem, avoid injuries,
achieve steady accomplishment, build
teamwork and camaraderie, and learn a lot
about baseball at every practice. You begin
by using games within the game of baseball
or softball and end with knowing how to
plan a full season of meetings and practice
sessions.

3 Checking the Equipment 27

Your first concern is the safety of your players. Properly used equipment can prevent many injuries.

4 Evaluating Your Talent 40

Every youngster on your team has to do certain things to play the game of baseball—run, bend, throw, and swing the bat. Your first job is to evaluate their present skill levels.

5 Throwing and Catching 45

The team that throws the ball accurately and catches it most of the time wins its share of games and, more important, enjoys the game more.

6 Hitting 60

"Know how" eliminates fear and gives sweet satisfaction and achievement in one of the most enjoyable acts in sports—smacking, powdering, smashing, connecting, blasting, meeting the ball. The fun increases as you teach your players how to get from first to second, to third and on home.

7 Pitching 81

The team with the best pitcher usually wins the game—and allows the best baseball to happen. When you teach pitchers under fifteen, you must know how to protect their arms from lifelong injury.

8 Catching—for the Catcher 95

Your catchers should be coached to know at least as much, if not more, about the game as any other player on the field.

9 Playing the Infield   105

You begin with catching and throwing and
end with what to do with the ball. Every hit
does not have to be an adventure.

10 Playing the Outfield   111

Beginning players can't all be put in right
field. Sooner, more often than later, the ball
gets hit to the outfield.

11 Managing and Coaching a Game   117

Buzz words, concentration, crowd and
parent management, and cooperating with
officials, opposing managers, and your
assistant coaches are some of the leadership
factors involved in letting each child play
the best he or she can. Your modeling will
last a lifetime.

12 For Your Clipboard   123

You can't remember everything! This
tear-out section lists the "buzz words" you
learned in the text. It will help trigger your
memory and aid your coaching on the field.

Foreword

I have spent almost every year of my entire life playing baseball, in a steady progression from sandlot to the pros. I started out in playground baseball, which preceded the Little League in our town, advanced to Little League, Pony League, American Legion, high school and college competition, went on to ten years of major league baseball, followed by ten (to this point) years of coaching and managing at the major league level. I had what I thought was a good background to coach successfully on any level. To my surprise I found I was not the all-knowing baseball expert and supportive father I thought I was.

My rude awakening occurred a few years ago as my middle son said his prayers one night with my wife. "I wish Daddy wouldn't yell so much at my games." Here I was thinking I was spurring on my son and his teammates, only to find out that I was embarrassing the one I wanted to help the most.

I should have started to get the message years before when my children were very young. I would get out in the yard to "play" with them and start to teach them baseball fundamentals and skills as we played. They would quickly tire of the instructional aspect and say, "We'd rather play with Mommy; she makes it fun."

There is so much involved in helping a youngster as he or she strives to master a game such as baseball, especially in a very organized, structured situation. Messrs. Aschermann and O'Shea have addressed this dilemma in this book: how does a coach help kids learn and develop without hurting them and without spoiling the fun they are out on the field for in the first place? They recognize that there is more to coaching than teaching. Their order of priorities is fun, learning, growing, and winning, in that order—not losing sight of the fact that kids should be striving to do the very best they can along the way. In a knowledgeable but sensitive, sensible, and humorous way, they convey their basic concern for the child's emotional and physical welfare. If these are dealt with, with tender loving care, the winning will follow; if the winning gets priority, the child's welfare tends to suffer, to the detriment of all.

What makes for a good, successful coach? Read this book and find out. It will heighten your awareness that, as a coach, it is a whole, feeling, impressionable child you are entrusted with, not just a baseball player. Your team will be the better for it, and you will be too.

—Jeff Torborg, New York Yankees Coach

Preface

This book is for you, the volunteer coach or parent who loves the game of baseball and enjoys working with youngsters, but may need some assistance in teaching the sport effectively and enjoyably. It's a book of basics, not a detailed skill level book. The skills, the drills, the teaching systems are designed to help you coach youngsters five to fourteen years old; to prepare you to take on a team and teach the basics while having fun.

This guide has grown out of the authors' association as youth league coaches, the needs we observed in our own towns, and the reactions of other coaches (both novice and experienced) to a series of live youth league coaching clinics we developed and presented in Yankee Stadium and other New York locations.

We come from different fields—Kurt Aschermann is a trained professional coach and Gerard O'Shea is a volunteer parent coach who is an educator—yet as "pro" and "dad" we share the same viewpoint about youth sports. We believe that the objects of youth sports on all levels are fun, learning, individual development, and winning—in that order. We make no secret of our feeling that the most important part of your job as coach is to make sure your squad has fun; the second most important part is to teach them all you can; third, to make sure they develop as individuals and as members of a team; and fourth, to win when you can. We're not suggesting that you overlook the importance of succeeding and winning—the coach who forgets to encourage the kids to strive as hard as they can to win is cheating his team—but learning to enjoy the game is more important.

In the beginning, the child and the coach each have a major fear. The child is afraid he will drop the ball or strike out and that will cost the team the game. The coach is afraid the team will feel he doesn't know enough. Whatever background or skill level you start with, you can overcome both fears with the suggestions and hints offered here. We will also be discussing rules and strategies we feel you must follow for the growth and safety of your squad. These are the same strategies we have demonstrated successfully at our Coaching Clinics: our buzz-word technique of instruction, games for your use in teaching and advancing basic skills, and suggestions on how to maintain and build your leadership. In short, we are offering the basics you should know to insure the learning, safety, and pleasure you and each child deserve when you all hear the cry each spring . . .

Play Ball!

1

Building the Team,
Child by Child

Whether the team you coach does or does not enjoy the season; whether or not they increase their love of baseball or softball depends on you, Coach, on your understanding of your players and your behavior toward your team.

Some of us remember when, as kids, we would go out to a field with a few friends and play ball all day. We'd stop only for lunch or when it got too dark to see. The score would be 153 to 147. Each of us would hit a dozen home runs, strike out thirty times, make a score of errors, catch our share, and learn from experience. No adults were present; somehow we had a good time without pressure. We played more in one week than kids practice and play today in a whole season.

Now our teams meet with us twice a week for an hour and a half, and we play a two hour game. As coach, you have a great deal to do in very little time. You'll find yourself tempted to pressure your players toward perfection. Resist the temptation. Remember, the most important thing you can teach is to share with each child your own enjoyment of the sport. One way to do this is to build in each child the feeling that he or she has learned something new each time you meet. It's a growth process and it takes patience.

Jeff Torborg, coach of the New York Yankees, said at one of our clinics in Yankee Stadium, "Be gentle with the kids. Let them enjoy the game. I played ten years in the major leagues for the Dodgers and the Angels. I had wonderful professional experiences. I caught three no hitters and a perfect game with Sandy Koufax. I have obviously had a wonderful and gratifying career in professional sports. But the coach I remember the most was the one who cut me from the seventh grade basketball team. My other coaches had a lot of making up to do. When you coach kids they need your demonstrative care to help them become strong adults."

THE BALL STOPS HERE

As a coach, you may find you need caring and support also. Some days you will plan a wonderful practice session only to find your team has decided this is the day to "get the coach." At some games, you may feel that every parent, neighbor, and official is on your back—you may feel like a cross between Joan of Arc and Abraham Lincoln in their final moments. On these days remind yourself that all projects have their ups and downs.

Whether you've always wanted to coach, whether you didn't know how to say "no," or whether you felt this was an ideal way to spend more time with your child, you are bound to have some apprehensions about how you will manage yourself and your team and how you will teach the necessary skills. Here, you may find it helpful to seek the assistance of your mate or a friend or neighbor who will still like you after the season is over. At least find someone you can talk to openly about your plans and accomplishments and your frustrations and disappointments. Other coaches you respect could be included on your abbreviated list of supportive persons. It is much easier to make your coaching decisions after you have explored and aired alternatives.

COACHING THE CHILD AND TEACHING NEW SKILLS

To teach a new skill, plant the seed well. You teach the skill and then make it a habit—that's where repetition comes in. It will be fun and more rewarding if the child succeeds measurably with the skill being taught, so start with the simple skills many of the youngsters may know already. Remember, children need to have a clear, readable goal they can achieve, within their abilities. They want you to describe and show them what you want them to do. Then, let them try it out; be sure to encourage each child to measure his or her own improvement and they will enjoy practice more. If they feel you are evaluating them, their intelligence, or their dexterity, you'll lose them.

Here's a way many experienced coaches approach skill development:

1. **Teach only one skill at a time.** Show and demonstrate first, then have the player do it.

2. **Let the player repeat it; repeat it again.** A good habit, as well as a bad one, is learned by repetition. A habit is nothing more than something you did once and then repeated again and again until you became the habit and the habit became you. You learn bad habits such as smoking and overeating the same way you learn good habits like standing straight and walking tall.

3. **Use suggestion.** Give the players a picture when

you can. Say, "It's like throwing stones into a pond. . . . It's like catching houseflies. . . . It's like balancing on a bar or a fence." All of us like pictures. Children are no exception.

4. **Judge and evaluate performance only, not the child.** Encourage the players to judge their progress based only on their own previous performance—their *own* performance, not their teammates'. Judge your progress as a coach the same way. A season is very long when you keep score by games won and lost. Your real challenge lies in how much better your players did today than yesterday. Compare yourself only to yourself. Let the children see you judge performance this way and they'll begin judging themselves the same way. Eventually, they will start judging their teammates that way. It's rewarding to hear one player saying to another, "That's the best you ever played. You caught the ball even better than last week."

5. **Be realistic.** All learning has highs and lows. When an individual player is having a good practice or game, praise him, but accurately. A pat on the back encourages your player, but overpraising can ruin a child's future performance. If you continually say, "Great!" "Fantastic!" "You're the best!" where can a child go from there except down? Exclaim rarely; show your pride often. "I'm proud of you. That's the best you've ever done that. . . . You worked very hard today," are more powerful in allowing learning and self-esteem to grow than are the exaggerated cliches.

6. **Plateauing and below-par performances.** When your player or team is playing or practicing below

par, be patient; don't panic. Regression and plateauing are part of integrating a skill. Watch how a child's skills develop. He will perform above and below his par over a measured period of time. Only after the level of excellence maintains itself at above par do you set that level as his new par. Compare each child to only one person—himself or herself.

Good practice makes good players. Bad practice makes a long season. If you work on the premise that *you become what you do,* you and your players will accomplish hundreds of goals and you will have much more to do than simply winning or losing games. You will have a winning season.

2

Planning a Meaningful Practice

Baseball is exciting but practice can be boring! There is probably nothing more boring in the entire world of sports than a poorly planned baseball or softball practice. All practices should be structured with active segments. A practice is doomed if players stand around waiting to do something. Fortunately, it doesn't have to be that way. If you spend some time organizing and planning your practices, they can be beneficial and fun for both you and the kids. The key to a good practice is to have a focus.

Let's take a look at a general practice outline.

1. **Hold a short meeting.** Start every practice with conversation. Sit the club down on the grass or in the bleachers and review the practice you had yesterday, talk about the practice to come, the game coming, the games past. Allow them to understand what you are going to teach them and why you are going to do it. This style of coaching encourages them to focus; it involves the child in developing his own skills.

2. Warm-up. Many injuries occur in sports because of inadequate warm-up. Here are a few stretching and bending exercises most of your players will know and which fill the warm-up bill perfectly.

JUMPING JACKS

They may not be modern, but they do the job. Arms and legs are extended on the count of one. Return hands to sides and feet together on two. Ten Jumping Jacks will do fine.

TOE TOUCHING/ARM EXTENSION

Stand erect with hands on hips to start. Extend arms high over head on the count of one. Keeping knees straight, bend from the waist and reach for toes on two. Return to standing erect with hands over head on three. Back to hands on hips on four. Ten times is enough for this one.

REACH TO THE ANKLE

Stand erect with feet separated. Reach right hand down to touch the top of the left leg on the count of one. Return to standing erect on two. Reach left hand down to touch the top of the right leg on three. Return to standing erect on four. Ten times is sufficient.

①

②

③

④   ⑤

HURDLER'S STRETCH

With one knee bent, extend the other leg and *slowly* stretch the extended muscles. Then switch sides.

There are others you may want to use for variety, like the Overhand Stretch or the Side Stretch. Just be sure you and your players have gently stretched all the muscles they'll be using when they play ball. Five minutes of these exercises is enough. Then let them jog around the infield to finish up.

Because children learn by example, you'll probably want to do the warm-ups with them; but if you work at a desk all day, be careful not to overdo—one or two rounds of each exercise is enough for you to start with; you can build up as the season progresses.

3. **Teach.** When you teach a new skill or develop a known skill, begin the practice with that skill. Do it right away while your players are fresh and enthusiastic. Position them so they can see the demonstration; don't talk too long—they'll be impatient to try it for themselves. Try not to teach more than one skill in a practice.

4. **Drill.** Immediately after you teach it, drill it. The drill you choose for the skill development should be fun. Bunt kickballs, or bunt with tennis rackets, hold a bunting scrimmage. You'll want to do something that teaches the skill without the child's necessarily knowing he's being taught. It's best to have activities where the children perceive they are enjoying themselves. It's natural at this age to play in order to learn.

5. **Have a "game."** After you have taught and after you have drilled, try to get the skill into competi-

tive game conditions immediately. For example, let's say you have been talking about fielding the ground ball. After teaching the proper technique (Chapter 5, page 56) and after hitting (or throwing) ground balls to each individual a few times (the drill part), try adding competition. Put out an infield and make everyone else on the team runners. **(Be sure to put helmets on the runners!)** As you hit a ground ball to the youngsters, have a runner run to first base. Obviously the infielders' job is to get him out. Count the outs versus the runs between the two teams; then switch the teams. You will find the enthusiasm is increased by keeping score because of the competition of playing a game.

Remember, the object is to have fun while developing the skill, so if a gimmick exists for that skill, use it. Consider the example above. You might want to go through the infield drill having the youngsters wear our famous wooden paddle instead of a glove. (See Chapter 5, page 59). Gimmicks are good as long as they teach new skills and reinforce good habits.

6. **Review.** Now, before you go on, review the skill. This is very important. Having had fun with the skill will often take away from its importance and the right way to do it. The joking and counting runs and laughing may make the players lose sight of why they are doing something. Review the skill with each child before doing anything else. Offer praise and encouragement.

7. **Compete.** Practice should end on a good note. Usually, the best way to insure a positive atmosphere is to end the practice with some competition. If you are following the skill/drill/compete

system, you may want to end with a short scrimmage.

8. **Warm-down.** Repeat warm-up exercises to guarantee muscles are relaxed again.

9. **Sit and talk again.** Before sending the youngsters home, review today's practice, yesterday's game, and tomorrow's game or practice.

10. **Physical check.** Check that all equipment is in playing shape. Ask the players if they feel sore any place. Observe them all the time—when they arrive, as they play, and at the conclusion. Look for favoring of a leg, rubbing of an arm. Review all our points on physical safety.

Planning and conducting good practice sessions will allow you to concentrate on the reason you and the children are there on the field. You will have prepared yourself to focus on certain skills; you'll look sharp and confident, and you will know what you are talking about. We have all had teachers or coaches who tried to bluff when they were not prepared. We knew they were bluffing; our respect for them suffered.

SUMMARY

1. Team meeting
2. Warm-up
3. Teach a skill
4. Drill the skill
5. Compete with the skill

6. Review the skill
7. Scrimmage
8. Warm-down
9. Team meeting
10. Physical check

3

Checking
the Equipment

Unfortunately, unlike the New York Yankees and the Chicago Cubs, nobody meets you on the first day of practice to ask you what equipment you need for the new season and which company you want to order it from. The fact is, on your first day the head of the league comes by and hands you a bag in which you find eight-year-old helmets, catching gear used by Yogi Berra thirty years ago, and bats that definitely have seen better days. Your problem is not which company to order from, but how you're going to make it through the season with what you have. Of course, you can attend the next league meeting and complain about the situation (and you should), but you're not likely to get anywhere. Let's talk about how you can manage.

Clearly, inadequate gear will cause problems. If your catcher is more worried about the fact that the chest protector touches the ground than how to catch the ball, you're going to have a lot of passed balls, but there are things you can do to make the equipment better and easier for your players to use.

Our rule for equipment is simple: make sure the stuff covers what it is supposed to cover *and is safe*. If your helmets have cracks in them or your shin guards are missing straps, it's going to make it harder for your team to play their best, and you are also running the risk of allowing unsafe use of that equipment. Injuries become more likely.

Let's go through the entire bag of equipment and talk about what you have to look for and what you can do to improve the equipment:

1. **Batting Helmets.** Most youth league programs now require that helmets be the double-flap style (both ears covered) and include a chin strap. If your helmets are not double ear flap—*don't use them! Get the right kind.* It's a safe bet that within a few years you will see even major leaguers wearing two-flap helmets that cover the whole head. This type is already being used on every other level of play, including the minor leagues.

Check the inside of the helmet carefully. Discard any helmet with a crack, as absolutely dangerous. You should also check to make sure the padding at the ear holes is there. If the padding on one side is missing or partially missing, obviously the helmet will not fit. This will cause it to turn as the player moves. Not only is this unsafe, but can you imagine trying to hit a fast ball while looking out through the earhole? Disconcerting, to say the least.

The chin strap is designed both to keep the helmet on the head while swinging or running and also to make it fit better. Chin straps can be a real advantage when you are issued only four sizes of helmets and you have ten different sizes of heads. Adjusting the straps will solve many of your problems.

Never use helmets that merely cover the side of the head. We used to call them "shells." Many leagues still use them as running helmets, but they should be banned. They provide the same protection as wearing nothing. If your league issues them, it's time to man the barricades, line up your votes, and storm the league meeting.

2. **Catching Gear.** The easiest way to explain how important it is to have catching gear that fits and is safe is to remind you of how your catcher became your catcher. Come on now, admit it. On your first day with your team you asked each player what position he plays and you had plenty of volunteers for each spot until you got to catcher. When you asked for catchers, you got blank stares. So how did you get a catcher? You drafted him by telling your choice that, "after all, if you're the only one, you'll get to play every game." Reminding yourself how your backstop became a backstop has to touch a nerve and help you realize that he is at a handicap already and the equipment he is required to wear shouldn't be an additional handicap.

Obviously, the catching gear has to be safe. You won't believe how fast you can lose a catcher; the first time your draftee gets one in the coconut and it hurts, you're going to be in the market for a replacement. So the equipment has to cover the body and provide the maximum protection possible. Let's take the pieces of equipment one at a time.

THE FACE MASK—There's nothing worse than throwing down to second base and having the face mask make a left turn south. Not only will your player look funny, but you'll find he spends more time worrying about the mask's fit than he does catching. You have to take the time to make sure the mask fits your catcher. Now we know how hard that can be during a youth league game. The umpire is in a hurry (after all, he feels he's underpaid and getting all the guff he can take), the other coach is in a hurry, your pitcher is in a hurry, and the last catcher was six feet tall with a size 7½ head. Taking time to readjust the mask is tedious and bothers some people. So what; take it! Take all the time you need to make sure you adjust those straps and make the mask fit the new player. You may upset some people, but you'll make your catcher happy and—even more important—safe.

There are two types of face masks: catcher's masks and umpires' masks. The catcher's mask is the wire type— more bars, heavier, and usually with side bars.

Umpires use the lighter single bar mask and your league probably does, too. There is little difference except weight, although you should check whichever one you have for cracks.

The one thing that should be required is the throat protector. That's the funny little piece of plastic that hangs from a couple of strings at the bottom of the mask. It serves the purpose of cutting off a foul ball before it hits the catcher in the Adam's apple. Ever been hit in the Adam's apple? There is no pain in the world like that one—it's the second most painful thing that can happen to a catcher. (Need we describe the first most painful?)

Make sure the mask fits, has a throat protector, and is light enough so your little rabbit catcher can keep his head up.

THE CHEST PROTECTOR—As we move down, we come to the chest protector. A loose or poorly fitting protector can drive your catcher nuts—and may drive your pitcher batty, too.

The chest protector should be fitted carefully and tightly, with the strap that holds it on the body going straight across the body without twisting into knots.

Old-fashioned chest protectors used to have an extension to protect the groin area. That style is harder to find today, but some manufacturers do make them and the additional protection is preferred for the younger grades. The bottom line, though, is that the chest protector should fit snugly, without cutting off circulation. In addition to the comfort factor of a tight chest protector, there is also the "more-safety-less-pain" factor. A chest protector snug against the chest does a better job of protecting your catcher from painful foul tips than a loose protector. Now, you may think this doesn't make sense because the loose one will give. You are half right—it does give, but it also hurts more when the ball makes contact. Try it yourself and you'll change your mind immediately.

THE GIRLS' CHEST PROTECTOR—Most women's chest protectors come with plastic inserts to protect the breast area. On the high school level, the girls seem to find them uncomfortable and remove them. They shouldn't. On the lower levels, there should be no flexibility—they should remain in the chest protector to cover the girl. Why risk the chance of injury, present or future, because of momentary discomfort? After two pitches, the discomfort will disappear and the girl will forget she has them in.

THE CUP—The rule here is simple. If you let your catcher go on the field without a protective cup, you are seriously endangering him. **No catcher should ever be allowed anywhere near a field without a protective cup.** For that matter, no male *player* should be allowed on the field without a protective cup. Let's repeat that for emphasis— **No male player should be allowed on the field without a protective cup.** Baseballs do not always go straight—and baseballs have a way of finding the vulnerable areas of an athlete. Those areas should be covered.

If you want to know how to get through to your players that they should wear a cup, use the example set by the major leagues. Tell them you know for a fact almost every single major league player wears a cup when he goes on the field. Do they really think a major league third baseman is going out there on artificial turf and have baseballs hit at him at 140 miles an hour without having a cup on? No way!

THE SHIN GUARDS—Shin guards can be the source of great discomfort for a catcher. If the shin guards are running up and down your catcher's legs, he will not be protected and he will worry a lot more about his legs than about catching the ball. There are three simple rules to follow:
• Get four-strap shin guards if you can. The fourth strap covers the top of the knee where most of the foul balls

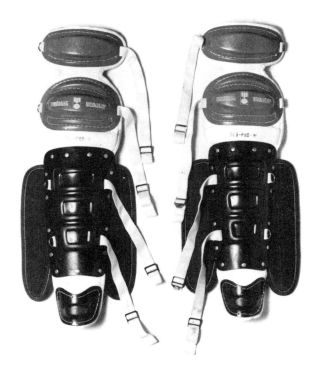

hit. Try to remember the last time you saw a catcher on any level get hit straight in the shins with a foul ball or a ball in the dirt. It very seldom happens. Most of the time, the catcher is hit on top of the knee. Bend over and notice what part of the leg is facing the pitcher—it's the top. The fourth strap on a shin guard covers this area.

• Never, never cross the straps behind the leg. We realize a few major leaguers cross the straps, but they shouldn't. After a while the crossed straps hurt and, even more important, they don't keep the shin guard on straight. Try this experiment with your catcher. Put the shin guards on with the straps straight and ask the player to bend his knee and bring his leg up. You will notice that the shin guard stays straight on his leg and therefore covers the entire knee. Now take the top strap and cross it with the next one down and do the same exercise. Notice how the top of the shin guard turns and leaves part of the knee exposed. Keep the straps straight.

• Try to get shin guards that have a leather extension on the side. This little piece covers that very vulnerable meaty part of the leg that usually gets hit when you get a pitch in the dirt.

The summary on the catching gear is clear: make sure the equipment is whole and fits the little body you're sending out there scared to death anyway. If he's protected correctly, injuries will not occur and he'll learn to love catching. If it doesn't fit, it's going to hurt and you will produce an outfielder.

That essentially covers the equipment that was handed to you from the league president. However, there are other pieces of equipment that must be checked *by you* to guarantee safety and to increase the success levels of your players.

3. **Other Equipment.** No discussion of equipment would be complete without spending some time on two items every player must have, and few coaches care about: the glove and the shoes.

GLOVE—Probably every coach has, at one time or another, been confronted by a player with a glove either too big, too small, or too beat up to be useable. Often the too-big glove results from the overzealous father who thinks his child is already Reggie Jackson and therefore should have Reggie Jackson's glove, right down to the size. Now, obviously, you can't influence the child or parent unless they ask. But you may be able to short circuit a couple of disasters by talking and demonstrating appropriate glove size and type before the season really gets under way. By all means, if the player asks for advice, give it freely and be specific— even go with the player to select a glove if you can. Success level will be drastically affected by glove size and condition.

The next problem the coach has is the whole question of conditioning and oiling the glove. Remember how we did it as kids? We'd get the new glove and oil it every night until it was nice and black and weighed fifty pounds. Today's gloves are not designed to be oiled extensively and a good coach will spend time early in the season instructing his players on proper oiling procedures. What works best is light oiling of the pocket twice per season and lightly oiling the back of the glove and the rawhide four or five times a season. You'll notice we suggest oiling the back more than the front since that part of the glove touches the ground (dirt) more and will dry out sooner. By the same token, time should be spent on the rawhide that holds the glove together. When a glove breaks, it's the strings holding it together that break first. If time is spent keeping them moist, they won't break as easily.

How do you break in a glove? Here you can use television as a tool of instruction. Suggest to your players that they watch TV and keep an eye on what the major leaguers do with their gloves before each pitch. What you and they will notice is that most pros break the glove *down* from the fingers to the pocket.

What we are trying to avoid is what most kids do—that is, break the glove *across*. What happens with the across break is that the glove loses its shape and causes your player to lose control. Try it. Grab a glove from one of your players and see if you can control it better when you break the fingers down. The other thing the down break does is put more surface on the field, where it is obviously needed.

Catchers, especially, should be encouraged to down break so they will have the greatest possible surface area

on the ground when they reach for balls in the dirt. By the way, there is nothing wrong with our old tried-and-true method of breaking in a new glove. Remember how we did it? Oil it, place a ball in the pocket, wrap with soft material to avoid cutting the leather (a torn T-shirt is best), and sleep on it. The player may not sleep well, but he will get a great pocket. Another way to speed up pocket development is to sit with a bat and pound the pocket.

SHOES—We're sure it's unnecessary to stress the regulation permitting only soft rubber or plastic spikes; no youth league permits metal spikes today. The new plastic spikes, shaped like the old metal ones, don't last as long, but they do work well. Many players now are switching to the Turf shoe, which has many little rubber cleats. They may look good, but they are designed to be used on "rugs," not dirt. Your player will not get as much traction from them as he will from the plastic spike or the molded sole.

It's important that you check every player's shoes before the season starts. You'd be surprised how your players' success levels can be affected by the condition of their shoes. Worn cleats can actually affect gait, missing tongues will certainly cause discomfort, and worn insides can force your players to run on the sides of their feet, which will slow them down and may even cause foot problems that will be felt at a later date and affect more than athletic ability. So, be sure you check those shoes and talk to the player's parents about any problems you observe. Very few parents will let their children continue to wear shoes that will hurt their feet and cause future miseries.

CLOTHING—Many youth leagues do not outfit their teams in baseball or softball uniforms as such. A numbered T-shirt is standard, with the rest frequently left to the family. Suggest appropriate clothing at your open meeting and/or in your preseason letter to parents. Long pants, warm-up or baseball-type pants, should be required. Shorts leave the legs too vulnerable to cuts and scratches.

A light jacket should also be *required equipment*, not just to temper brisk spring afternoons and evenings, but also to protect your players' warmed-up muscles. And of course your pitcher, the one person who is constantly moving, should never be off the field without wearing a jacket. This includes any time spent on the basepaths. Watch TV!

HATS—Ventilated visor caps will keep your players cooler under the sun and will shield their eyes from direct sunlight or night field lights. They should be worn for both practice and games. Most leagues issue the adjustable style that gives each player a good fit.

FIRST AID KIT—Scrapes and bruises do occur and you really should never be on the field without some basic medical supplies. You don't need anything elaborate; after all, 99 percent of your injuries will be very minor and most of them can be taken care of with a little ice or a bit of disinfectant and a Band-Aid.

The general rule here is I.C.E.—ice, compression, elevation. Most strains, bumps, and bruises should be treated with ice first. The object is to keep the blood away from the injury, so most of the time you are safe in applying ice right away. Then, the ice should be held firmly to the injury (compression) and the injured part of the body should be elevated if possible.

Your first aid kit should include: ice packs, Band-Aids, a disinfectant for cuts, gauze, tape, and elastic bandage. If the child needs more than that, he probably needs professional medical attention and should be treated immediately. (Remember, first aid is just that—*first* aid!) You should also have the telephone numbers of a doctor and/or the ambulance corps, the police, and a hospital taped to your clipboard. A quarter or two taped to the clipboard is also a good idea, along with a knowledge of the location of the nearest phone. Remember this rule: **when in doubt after an injury, call for help.**

WATER—It's a good idea to bring a jug of water or juice and paper cups to a practice or game. Leaving it to chance that a working water fountain will be a permanent fixture at every field is an optimistic viewpoint. Supplying your own refreshment has other advantages. Your team will be at hand for your coaching and teaching suggestions and concentrating on the practice or game instead of standing on a water fountain line at some other spot. You will also be able to monitor the amount of liquid your children are consuming. Liquid consumption during games and practices is necessary, since the body needs to replace the fluid it has lost through perspiration. Don't expect thirst to determine when and how much your players should drink. The fact is, a player's thirst is easily satisfied, often before full replenishment takes place. Be sure your team takes scheduled and required water or juice breaks throughout each practice or game, especially in hot weather, when the body loses fluid faster.

We suggest you assign an adult to bring and manage the juice or "water hole" at each game. Cookies or other treats are also well received at the end of a practice or game.

MEASURING ROPE—Setting up for practice will be easier if you measure out a sixty-foot piece of rope or strong twine, put a knot at the forty-five-foot mark, wrap it around a stick and carry it in your equipment bag. Whenever you need to set out bases or measure off the distance between the mound and home plate for your pitchers to warm up, just pull out your measuring rope and you'll have the exact distances immediately.

4

Evaluating Your Talent

Now, you have your team; you have the roster; you have the children standing before you. What's next? Many coaches begin with batting practice and infield practice and start to teach the system they intend to use. At this point, you're not ready to do that.

Let's think about the situation this way. Let's say this is your new job and the boss has taken you to your office, introduced you to your staff and defined the job you have to do. What would you do first? Most of us would evaluate the staff and try to determine what everybody is doing or can do. Your ball club needs the same evaluation.

Every youngster on your team has to do certain things to play the game of baseball: run, run laterally, run backward, bend, throw, and swing the bat. Our suggestion is that you use the first day to evaluate every player in each one of these skills. Only then will you be able to determine which ones are best, which ones are worst, and which ones are in between. And, after this careful evaluation, you will have an automatic practice system for teaching skills, reviewing skills, and honing skills.

Keeping in mind that you have limited time, limited resources, and limited field space, here's a simple test that will give you, in a short fifteen minutes or so, a complete check list on every player's skill levels and give you a good idea about the positions each child can best handle at this time. Let's take a look at it based on each of the skills mentioned above. All you'll need is a clipboard, pencil, paper with six boxes after each player's name, and a watch.

RUNNING—The simplest way to test them is to run them; obviously, if you use a watch with a second hand you will get some idea of who is fastest. But what you really want to look at is not their speed, but their *form*. As their coach and teacher, you will be instructing them on good running form, which will not only improve speed, but will also improve balance, turning power, and control. Here's what to look for:

1. Are the arms and hands close to the body and moving back and forth?
2. Are the arm movements corresponding to the leg movements (i.e., opposites at the same time)?
3. Are the legs and arms really pumping?
4. Where are the elbows? More players swing their elbows out than you can imagine. As the arms and elbows go out, gait is affected and body motion will slow.
5. Is the child leaning slightly forward? Probably no need to belabor this one—after all, have you ever seen a track star run standing up? Of course not. The object is to get the body moving forward in the direction in which it is intended to go.
6. Most important—are the feet straight and is the child landing on his toes? If the toes are pigeoned or flayed outward, it will affect both control and speed. At the

same time, children should be taught early that running on the toes is faster than on the heels, does far less damage to the legs, and *keeps the head and eyes straighter.* That means it will be easier for them to concentrate on the baseball when they chase it.

Rate each player on running form.

A large part of the game of baseball is running. You can improve the play of your team by drilling them in good running form at every practice.

LATERAL MOVEMENT—The fact is, players run laterally or at angles almost more than they run straight. All that's required here is to teach the child to go laterally from place to place without crossing feet and without falling.

It can be tested by simply marking two points on the field and timing each child to see how many times he can go between the two points in a specific period of time, say fifteen seconds. The simple way to improve lateral running is to teach side straddle hops without crossing the feet. (See Chapter 9 on infield play.)

Another great lateral movement drill, which is great for getting in shape and for cardio-vascular fitness, is the age-old baseball drill called "Pickups." The drill calls for one baseball and two players about ten feet from each other. One player rolls the ball to the side of the drilling player who side straddles to it, picks it up, and tosses it back, immediately after which he heads back in the other direction and retrieves the ball again. Tosses should be about fifteen or twenty feet and the drilling player has to be careful not to cross his feet. Another way to do it is the Long Pickup, which uses the same principle except that the drilling player actually runs and the distance between tosses is about fifty feet. Either way, your players will drill in lateral movement and get in shape.

Rate each player.

BACKWARD MOVEMENT—You may feel that except for a fly ball over the head and occasional backing up on a ground ball, there is very little need to move backward in a baseball game. But, how about when the pitcher must field a bunt, turn, and throw behind himself to first or second? Or, how about an outfielder going to the wall or backing up another player? And wait, how about that high fly ball that blows backward and has to be caught in a retreating position? If you watch the game, you'll see more backward movement than you thought possible. How do you test it? Run your players backward and time them. Run them backward, forward, and backward again to check for balance. After you have observed balance, you may want to toss a ball to them.

Rate each player on speed, control, and straightness.

Now that you have tested, how do you teach backward running? Refer back to the section on Running Form and reverse the process. Then, when your team is practicing sprints, run some of them backward. One thing more—explain why you are having your players do this. Remember, they will be more interested in doing it right if they know *why* they are doing it. This is a good rule for everything you teach.

Rate your players on backward movement.

BENDING—In addition to running, the other skill (we call it a skill on purpose) that every player must possess is bending. Just think of the times bending is necessary—fielding a ground ball, fielding a bunt, a low throw, a ball in the dirt, a low line drive, an errant throw, and more. So here we have another skill that's done constantly, yet few coaches teach it.

Let's test it first. Roll the ball to a player and ask that he bend and get it. Did he bend his knees? Did he keep his head down? Did he put his hands out in front with his body in control? And finally, was he in control enough to do something with the ball after picking it up?

Rate your players.

Now, let's teach bending. Line up the club and have them put their hands on their hips. Have them bend at the waist and knees. Check their form. Are they really bending their whole bodies? Again. Keep doing it until you are happy with the form and every player can bend according to your rules of bending. (Remember, children can learn while having fun. If this seems funny, make it funny, but keep things in control.) Now have them take their hands off their hips and reach out as they bend. Are the elbows in? Are the hands out? Are they bending at the knees and waist? Are their heads up?

Bending. An important part of the game and one that deserves at least thirty seconds a day of practice.

THROWING; SWINGING A BAT—Both of these skills can be tested by doing them: throwing the ball to a position with accuracy and swinging the bat without the ball (or from a batting tee). Proper procedures for each of these skills are in Chapters 5 and 6, so we won't go through it now, but you should look at each child before you start the season to check for blatant problems.

Rate your players on control and form.

SUMMARY

All the skills you will be teaching will be a combination of the basic skills we have discussed in this chapter. You have to know how each child performs these basic skills before you ask them to combine skills to play baseball or softball. Without this knowledge, you will be groping in the dark when you try to add a new dimension or simply diagnose why a child is not ready to play certain positions.

5

Throwing and Catching

The team that throws the ball more accurately and catches it more often is the team that wins the most. Sound basic? It is! The games of baseball and softball are games of throwing and catching, yet too many youth league coaches do not spend enough time on these two fundamental skills.

Spend time on the correct mechanics of throwing and catching during each and every practice and before games, and you will guarantee increased success levels for every child and the team. The corollary rule is: Perfect practice makes perfect, not practice alone. Let's consider these basics:

1. Conduct your throwing and catching drills with the players spaced no more than ten feet apart. It is very difficult to teach a skill when your players spend more time running after the ball or picking it out of the dirt than they do practicing.
2. Throwing and catching drills should be conducted at first without gloves. Two things happen

when you omit the gloves: a) the ball will be thrown more softly, giving the thrower better control, and, b) in order to succeed, the players will have to concentrate more, especially on the catching side.

3. No talking should go on during the warm-up or throwing/catching drills. The only voice your players should hear is yours—coaching, encouraging, and correcting. Your players will learn safely and correctly.

4. As with most skills, the more body movements you can eliminate while teaching, the less chance you have for error. When you are talking about arm elevation and shoulder rotation, described in this chapter, the best way to guarantee these elements will be learned is to eliminate the leg movement.

All initial throwing and catching drills should begin in the "knees down" position first. From there you can progress to one leg up, and then standing.

Throughout the chapters on teaching skills, we will suggest certain "buzz words" for you to use with your team. Buzz words, as we use them, are key words or phrases that will allow your players to receive a clear picture of the skill or rudiment as you first teach it. In later games and practices, your buzz words can be used to communicate quickly, quietly, and with sharp simplicity.

THROWING—If you concentrate on teaching the following four things, you will build correct throwing skills in your players. Let's look at the basic components of the good throw:

The grip

Arm elevation

Shoulder rotation

Follow through

Always remember, you're not teaching the college short-stop to make the throw from the hole or the minor league catcher to throw to second base. You're helping each one of your youth league players to throw the ball with more power, more accuracy, and more safety.

THE GRIP—Have you ever talked with your team (pitchers not included) about how to grip the ball? Very few coaches do. Did you ever ask yourself why there are stitches on the ball? The simple reason is that the stitches are there to make the ball move and give the thrower something to hold on to. Major league pitchers get movement on the ball *purely based on grip!* By the same token, major league catchers try to remove movement based on the grip they use on the ball. Remembering that you are trying to teach accuracy in throwing, you should be spending time ex-plaining and demonstrating how to hold the ball.

You have a couple of problems here: a) usually you're talking about little hands; and with little hands, your players have enough trouble getting any kind of grip on the ball in any way, let alone in a prescribed way; b) you have to consider that if you spend too much time talking about the proper way to hold the ball, your players may start thinking too much and acting too little and too late. (Just picture your shortstop fielding a hot smash and taking ten minutes trying to figure out how Coach told him to hold the ball.)

Now let's talk about where to put the hand on the ball. Too often, youth league players throw a baseball like a football (i.e., with the "V" of the palm facing the back and the fingers on the side of the ball). When the ball is thrown this way, a) the power the player gets behind the ball is drastically reduced, and b) accuracy is diminished because there is less surface area behind the ball.

Teach your players to hold the ball across the fat part of the seams. With this grip there will be backward rotation on the ball and therefore less movement. Teach keeping a space between the ball and the palm of the hand. This will allow for more power and force behind the ball. Teach keeping the hand on top of the ball and behind the ball, where it belongs. This will improve both accuracy and power.

The buzz words here are **HAND BEHIND THE BALL.** All you should be teaching, after you have talked about grip, is that the hand, meaning the palm and fingers, should be behind and therefore on top of the ball.

Remember, you can't just tell your players to do something; you have to explain to them why you want them to do it.

ARM ELEVATION—About 90 percent of your players are probably throwing incorrectly from the start, holding the elbow below the shoulder. Ask yourself what happens when your players throw with the elbow below the shoul-

der. They get much more rotation on the ball! The accuracy will be diminished. Teach your players to keep their elbows above their shoulders. Your buzz word for this could be **ELBOW UP.** Just mentioning this should trigger a mental picture that will remind your players to get their elbows above their shoulders.

SHOULDER ROTATION—Watch the major leaguer. Very seldom do you see a major leaguer throw the ball without turning his shoulders in the direction the ball is intended to go.

In this sense, the throw is like the tennis swing or the golf swing. The shoulders are turned so that both power and accuracy are improved. The key to teaching shoulder rotation is to make sure the motion is exaggerated. Dur-

ing drills and warm-up, the coach should make sure that the players are really turning all the way around when they throw.

THE FOLLOW-THROUGH—There is probably little need to discuss follow-through in depth because most youth league coaches are well aware of the need for the pitcher to follow through for best control and power. But, how often do we stress the follow-through to the other players on the field? Probably not nearly enough. The mechanics of throwing correctly dictate that everyone should follow through for accuracy and momentum.

Here are some drills to teach the proper skills of throwing. *Remember, keep your players fairly close together.*

Start everyone with a partner, a baseball, and no gloves. Place the players in two straight lines facing each other. (Note: all warm-up drills should be conducted this way, with everyone throwing in the same direction.) After your lines are established, place all players on their knees facing each other.

Drill 1—Begin tossing the ball back and forth (about ten feet) and exaggerate good shoulder rotation, hand behind the ball, elbow extension, and follow-through. (They should touch the ground when following through in this position.)

Remember, no one talks but the coach. No talking by players at all during the drill. You want to stress the discipline of concentration and the discipline of the coach having the opportunity to instruct.

Watch your players carefully. Are they turning? Are they behind the ball? Are they following through with the elbow up? Walk behind the line; coach and talk to each player. "Good, John. Good arm elevation." "More shoulder rotation, Mary." "Bill, let me show you how to put your hand behind the ball."

The rest of the drills follow the same pattern. Progress through these positions, always watching, always instructing:

Drill 2—Same drill, with the throwing leg up.
Drill 3—Same drill, standing—no stride.
Drill 4—Same drill, with a stride.
Drill 5—Same drill, with gloves.
Drill 6—Same drill, move back.
Drill 7—Same drill, with back leg on a chair for follow-through extension.

Simple, isn't it? If you spend a few minutes of each practice doing these drills you will improve the throwing accuracy and strength of all your players. These are the only throwing drills you have to do! The repetition and constant reminder of these simple warm-up drills will teach the skill.

PLAY "21"—To make a game of these drills, play "21." "Twenty-one" is a simple game in which the partners keep score against each other. A throw that is a "direct hit" to the chest of the other player is worth two points; a "direct hit" to the face is worth one. The first player to reach twenty-one wins.

Okay, Coach, you've taught them how to throw it. Now all you have to do is get someone to catch it!

CATCHING—Don't just assume your players can catch the ball. They have to be taught the skill like any other. You can do this by concentrating on five areas:
1. Movement
2. Extension
3. Bending
4. Thumbs and pinkies
5. Drills

Let's look at each component separately; then, we'll put them all back together again.

MOVEMENT/USING TWO HANDS—Kids don't move! We believe television has contributed a good deal to their stillness. Our kids have been watching the one-handed grabs highlighted on the tube so often they think it's cool and correct to catch a ball that way. When we were kids we knew it was cool, but we also knew it was incorrect. You must teach your players to move to the ball and use two hands to catch it.

The rules here are simple. If you can get your body in front of the ball, do so. You will be as surprised as your players how often the stab or reach is unnecessary because there is time to get in front of the ball. Once in front of the ball, use two hands to catch it at all times.

EXTENSION—The ball that goes "through the wickets" on your shortstop usually does so because your player has waited for the ball to get to him and has allowed the ball to go too far between his legs.

Teach extension of the arms out in front of the body to catch every thrown and hit ball. With the arms out, your player accomplishes several things. Obviously, he gets the ball sooner (how many times does the runner beat the throw to first because your first baseman caught the ball against his body?) and by extending his arms the ball is "cushioned" or "cradled" better, which leads to increased

control. On the ground ball, extension is even more important because it keeps the ball in front of the fielder and
also allows time to recover if the ball should bounce off his
body and land in front. He will often still have time to
make the play.

BENDING—If you've read other texts on playing baseball,
you may wonder why none of them mentioned bending.

The texts you've read are probably much more advanced than you need; remember that you're dealing with a youth league team. Your kids don't bend over! Watch them when they throw and catch. You'll see that they bend slightly, bend not at all, or just extend their arms. This is a skill you'll need to teach and practice. Stress to your youngsters that they have to bend from the waist and knees in order to get in front of the ball.

THUMBS AND PINKIES—(This one may get a big laugh at the coaches' meeting.) It simply means that every ball above the waist should be caught with the thumbs together and every ball below the waist with the pinkies together.

It's a simple concept that works, and it provides somewhat amusing buzz words that will immediately call to the players' minds what you are talking about. The first time your left fielder comes in for a bouncing ball holding his glove with thumbs together and you yell, "That ball was a pinkies!" you'll see what it does for the laughter level on the field. But, your fielder and every player on your club will know exactly what you're talking about.

DRILL—You shouldn't need to teach anything else about catching the ball except these basic skills, but you *do* have to teach them. And after you have talked about them and taught them, you must drill them.

- Quick movement drill without gloves or ball. Simply run your players from point to point. (Not too far, you're teaching quickness and movement, not endurance.) Place something on the ground, start the player at another point, yell "go" and watch his or her movement to the other point, finishing with a bend. Once you are comfortable with the movement without equipment, add the ball only.

  From here, of course, progress to movement with glove and ball. (**Note:** Remember, most balls thrown to your players are not thrown straight. All drills should be taught and practiced with the ball thrown more errantly than accurately.) Remember also to move them forward and backward. Watch their feet! You don't want them to cross their feet when going from side to side unless the distance requires it.

- The best drill for teaching catching is to throw the ball at them. Go back a couple of pages to the throwing drills that start on the knees and finish standing with full extension. Although you'll require that everyone concentrate on *both* throwing and catching, you might want to start your drill by deciding one line will throw and the other will catch; later, reverse the positions. That way you, too, can concentrate on the skill at hand. Make sure the errant throw is included so the players can work on catching it.

Wooden paddle drill. Take a piece of plywood and cut a circle ten inches in diameter. Tack or staple a work glove on one side. You now have in your possession the finest and cheapest piece of teaching equipment ever invented for the game of baseball or softball.

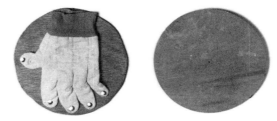

Put a paddle on the glove hand of each player and ask them to play catch. You'll notice immediately the players stop using one hand to catch—they simply can't with the paddle. Watch how they move to get in front of the ball so they can catch with both hands. (It's a great teaching tool, but be sure that the players using the paddles are careful. The ball can bounce off the paddle and hit body parts. Following the suggestion of staying close together for drill will solve the problem.)

SUMMARY

You can teach throwing and catching by using simple drills, demonstrations, and explanations. If you take the time to practice these basic skills of the game, the harder and more complex skills will fall into place for your players.

6

Hitting

Somewhere, sometime, somebody said, "Hitting the baseball is the single most difficult thing to do in sports." Whoever said that knew what he was talking about. Hitting that little round ball with the round bat is tough! Are good hitters born or made? That's harder to answer, a good case can be made either way.

However, as a youth league coach, you shouldn't worry about that. On the level you are teaching, *every* one of your players can be improved. Even your best hitter can get better.

One thing we are constantly asked at our Baseball/ Softball Clinics is to discuss the difference between the Charlie Lau and Ted Williams theories of hitting. Both of these men have had unbelievable success with their hitting instruction and therefore there is honest disagreement about their divergent styles. Simply stated, the Lau method emphasizes weight distribution, starting back and finishing forward; the Williams method emphasizes that the weight should start back and stay back. The rest of their hitting technique is basically the same. Usually, youth league coaches ask, "What style should we teach?"

The answer encompasses the key to our entire philosophy of teaching: if what the player is doing works and he is successful with his method, leave him alone. After you have read this chapter you will have learned the basic components of hitting that every good hitter includes in his style. What the child does after that in terms of idiosyncrasies or personal style is irrelevant, so long as he does the job and hits the ball. So, forget all these theories of hitting. On this level we essentially want to teach every player the same rudiments of hitting the baseball.

Don't change a player's style because of your own personal biases or theories; *but,* if what he is doing will hurt him physically or will have to be changed by some other coach later in his baseball career, change him now. An example here may better explain this point. Johnny is your best hitter. You can always depend on him to get the hit when you need it; to drive in that run you need, etc. Only one problem—Johnny hits all of his frozen ropes while stepping in the bucket. He hits the ball hard, but when the ball is thrown on the outside of the plate he has trouble reaching it. On our level, that doesn't happen too often and usually during his time at bat he's thrown one to the inside and he hits a rocket to right field, even though he steps in the bucket.

As coach, you have a tough decision to make. If you change Johnny now, you probably will reduce his success level drastically. If you change him now and he doesn't succeed, he's going to blame you and maybe even stop playing because he will have gone from hero to regular, ordinary hitter. Tough one, Coach.

There are a couple of things you could do and the easiest way out is to do nothing. However, we feel you should meet this problem head on. If you don't correct him now, someone will have to later, and as he gets older the chances of his changing and *his ability to change* are drastically reduced. You are actually doing this player a grave disservice if you do not change him. There is, of course, a proper way to do it. You have to explain it to him and probably to his parents. You may have to explain it to the entire team as well, so they will understand. It's tough, but it has to be done if you are really interested in Johnny's baseball development.

HITTING: THE STANCE

Stance is your first focus. Alas, if there is one skill television cannot help you with, it is batting stance. The only thing your players will see on television is that every player has his own style. Stress that it's a mistake to copy someone else. No two people can do the same thing out of the same position. There are, however, certain components of the stance and hitting mechanics that are generally uniform. Even though the entire body is involved in hitting the baseball, let's explain each of these by talking about body parts separately.

HANDS—Most of your kids hold the bat incorrectly. Look at their hands and what you will see is that they hold the bat back in the "crotch" of the palm as if they were cutting wood with an axe.

Try this simple test. Paint the end of a bat, the absolute end. Hand it to one of your players and ask him to take a very slow swing. You'll notice something very quickly: with the bat held back in the palms, the end is forced to rise ever so slightly when he swings. (What happens is that the wrists lock and for them to break on the swing, he has to raise the bat.) Try it yourself. Now try the grip shown below, with the bat held in the finger tips. Make sure the second knuckle is lined up on both hands.

INCORRECT   CORRECT

Feels strange, doesn't it? But take the same swing and you'll notice that the wrists break quite easily and the bat head does not rise. And something else—this grip places both palms behind the bat—a sure way to increase power. How about that!

If you can get your hitters to use this grip (and it won't be easy because it feels terrible in the beginning) they will get more wrist into the ball, more power in the stroke and, most important of all, more level swings. It just has to improve success levels. If your players look carefully at the major leaguers on TV, they'll notice most of them hold the bat this way. Remember, line up knuckle number two.

HANDS/ELBOW—The logical thing to talk about at this point is what happens on the other end of those hands. When we were kids, every coach taught "elbow up." No doubt that's the way you were taught, too.

Let's analyze this. Go back to that slow swing we talked about before and do it again. This time, keep an eye on your elbow and arm. Notice that in order to initiate the swing you actually had to make three different arm movements: a) you had to bring the elbow down, b) you had to bring the bat down so it was level in the hitting zone, and c) you had to initiate arm motion to begin the swing. Now let's recall what we said in the previous chapter—if you can eliminate unneeded body movements in developing a skill, you will reduce the chance of mistakes.

What's all this leading up to? It seems you and I were taught incorrectly. The results are better if the elbow is *down*, approximately six inches from the side, with the bat straight up. Let's try the swing again: a) bring the bat down, and b) initiate the swing. We have eliminated one potential problem and we have gotten the bat down into the hitting zone more rapidly. Try this and you will find faster bats and fewer pop ups.

Incidentally, coaches often say they want the elbow up to prevent the player from "hitching" before he swings. Just the opposite really happens: by having the elbow up, you are encouraging your player to hitch. Look at it this way—the player has to bring the elbow down to initiate the swing, doesn't he? Find one ten-year-old who can drop his elbow *without dropping his hands* and we'll show you a future superstar! It's just too difficult for kids to do this. When that elbow goes down, so will the hands, and that's the hitch.

FEET—Let's get the closed-versus open-stance question out of the way first. A closed stance has nothing to do with how far apart the feet are; it has to do with their relative position to each other. In a closed stance for a right hander, the left foot is in front of the right.

In an open stance the left foot is behind the right.

Which stance is best? Neither. In our opinion, the best way to teach a child to hit is to start with the feet parallel.

Every time a player shifts his feet up or back he is compensating for something. It may be eyes, bat speed, foot speed, or something else; but if he is compensating, he is doing something wrong and the antidote is to fix the mistake instead of forgetting it and working around it.

EYES AND CHIN—The hard truth is that if the player doesn't see the ball, he certainly isn't going to hit it. And the fact is that most of your players are probably trying to hit the ball with only one eye looking at it. Try this simple test. Stand straight, but look to one side with your eyes only. What's in the way? Did you notice that dark area you seem to be looking through? It's your nose—and it's in the way! Your youngsters look at the pitcher in essentially the same position and therefore are actually using only one eye to see. Doesn't it make sense that any object you put in the way of their seeing the ball is going to make it harder to see?

How do you stop it? First, let each member of your team try the same test for himself. You'll be surprised at what a revelation this is to your players. To correct the problem, teach them the shoulder-to-shoulder system. Have each player put their chin on their leading shoulder while in the batting-stance position and make sure both eyes can see the pitcher.

Now have them slowly swing the bat (or imaginary bat) and finish with their chin on the other shoulder. (We have asked the players in these pictures to exaggerate their head placement so you can see what we mean.)

Two things will happen if you teach head movement this way when hitting: a) both eyes see and follow the ball and b) the age-old problem of pulling the head out is eliminated. At the same time, you have taught almost all you have to about hitting on youth league level because you yourself know that the biggest problem in hitting on this level is pulling the head out on the swing.

You are now mechanically set up to hit. Stance and body position are established and you are following the general rule about not changing a player who hits well unless he or she is doing something that will physically hurt him or her or something that will have to be changed later. Now let's talk about the swing and the drills you can use to teach your players to be better hitters.

HITTING: THE SWING

The Charlie Lau theory of weight distribution seems more workable for young players. The weight must start back on your little rabbits to help them *control* their bodies. After all, you know that holding back or kicking off the swing are very difficult things for little people to do. Therefore, start them with their weight slightly back so they have a head start on keeping weight under control.

THE STRIDE—This is the toughest part to teach. Not too far, not too short, but just right. What is just right? Simply put, the correct stride for each player is the stride that allows him to remain in control of his body. How do you test the stride? Have each youngster take his stride and hold it. Then you, Coach, walk up (either in front of him or behind him) and give him a slight push. If he topples over, the stride is probably too long; if he is like a rock and immovable, the stride is too short. What you are looking for is that good, old-fashioned happy medium.

An important part of that happy medium involves the feet; like Ted Williams, your player should be facing the pitcher when he finishes his swing.

HIPS—By opening his hips to the pitcher, he will swing a stronger bat, see the ball better, and get all the necessary parts of the body moving at the same time. The key here is to make sure your players are not locking their hips and thus hitting the ball over home plate instead of getting the head of the bat out to make contact just in front of the plate. This is the one skill in hitting you must teach, drill, teach, drill and drill again. *If the hips are locked the player will never, never be a good hitter.*

HANDS—Finally, let's talk about what to do with the hands both during and after the swing. The major league norm today seems to be to let go of the bat with the back hand on the theory that once contact is made the back, or push, hand is kind of useless anyway and not needed. We have mixed emotions about this, but believe that on youth league level the youngsters should be taught to control the bat; they can control it better with both hands on it from start to finish. Therefore, you should teach hitting that way; but don't be too dogmatic about it if you have someone who does everything right but doesn't hold onto the bat with both hands.

The bottom line is that you want control, power, and follow-through. By combining these components, you will get them.

HITTING: DRILLS

Nothing beats good old batting practice. No drill, gimmick, or idea works better than actually putting the youngsters up there swinging the bat against live pitching. The more of this you can do, the better. (A word of caution here. Nothing is worse for teaching hitting than making the batter feel as if he is at Pearl Harbor with the word "Arizona" painted on his side. You know what we mean—batting practice with a pitcher who cannot consistently throw the ball over the plate at a moderate speed.) If you don't have a pitcher who can throw strikes, throw batting practice yourself. The best batting practice pitcher is the coach, although your arm may head south before the season is over if you throw during every practice. Try recruiting some of the parents to help here. It will be worth the trouble to know that your kids are hitting pitching instead of the pitching hitting them.

This doesn't mean you shouldn't try new pitchers—everybody on your team should try pitching—and every pitcher should practice with live batters. Just don't call it batting practice.

Keep the number of swings each player gets to a minimum to prevent the children from getting bored and the hitter from getting tired. You'll be much better off giving them ten swings and going around twice than letting them take twenty swings at once. And, since you want to make every part of batting practice worthwhile, be sure the entire club is concentrating on playing their positions in the field. The best defensive drills in the world can't do what actually playing the ball off the bat does.

Think safety. Remember the batting helmets. Remember that if something else is going on at the same time, it must happen *between pitches* so that every player can concentrate on the ball and the batter.

SHORT TOSS—This is an excellent batting practice drill. It is also the simplest and one that you can do with all your players at the same time. Look at the diagrams on facing page:

Note that the coach is slightly in front of the batter and is set to toss the ball so it lands on a certain spot on the ground if missed. This lets the batter time his swing and make contact with the ball at the same place each time. Let the coach simply short-toss the ball slowly toward the batter to give him time to adjust to each toss. The batter does what he would do in any hitting drill—he hits the ball. (The best place to do this drill is against a fence or screen so you don't have to retrieve the balls.) In this simple drill the hitter can hit a bucket of balls without taking too much time and the coach is there to correct his mistakes. Only a coach or assistant should do the tossing.

Do not allow a child to do the tossing. Indeed, children should never be too near a player with a bat. A flying bat or hit ball can cause serious injury. Team members should be a safe distance away in the field or behind the screen.

THE BATTING "T"—This is a tool you probably have seen. It is simply a rubber hose on the end of a plate-like base. The "T" is designed to work on the mechanics of hitting because it allows the batter to swing at a stationary object. Remember, the ball should be set on the "T" slightly forward of the batter because you are trying to teach hitting the baseball in front of home plate. You will defeat your purpose if you set the "T" up directly opposite the batter. A good way to do this is to place a home plate in back of the "T."

The best way to use the "T" is to allow the player enough time to hit a lot of baseballs. It can also be used in a scrimmage. As a matter of fact, quite a few youth leagues start their younger children on a "T" during games.

THE RUBBER HOSE—This item may seem a little weird. Take a look at the hose in the diagram and note that it is a simple piece of garden hose with one end taped.

The drill is simple. The coach holds the hose on one end and the players hit the other end as if it were a baseball. Notice how much control you have here, Coach. You are close enough to the hitter to watch his swing and you can even control where the "pitch" is. A word of caution: the hose can get loose and may hit someone when insufficient control is exercised. The coach, and only the coach, should hold the hose for the hitters.

BUNTING—(Not all youth leagues allow bunting, so make sure yours does before taking the time to teach it.) If you teach your team to bunt by the square-around method you're asking them to face the pitcher and make contact with the ball in an unfamiliar position. Because the pitching your players see in the early years can be less than controlled, your kids could get hurt. Here's a way of teaching bunting that is simpler and incorporates the usual way your player sees the ball. You may be surprised to know this is also the way professionals are taught to bunt. Instead of squaring, teach your youngsters to pivot at the hips.

Note that the bunter still faces the pitcher, but not with his body open. The arm extension, with his back hand at the label and his forward hand at the nob, is the same.

Your player bends at the knees, extends his arms, and keeps the bat at letter height. (This way, anything above the bat is automatically a ball and can be taken.) The object here is simply to make contact with the ball. Don't worry about *where* the player puts the ball down; just teach getting it down. On your level you have only one purpose: move the runner over by bunting. Teach sacrifice; remember, that's what it's called for a reason. The object is to give yourself up to advance the runners.

Repetition works best. After instructing your team in bunting, drill them by short-tossing the ball at the batter from a near distance—ten feet is fine to start. As confidence develops, increase the length of the toss until you're throwing from the mound to home plate.

BASERUNNING

No discussion of hitting would be complete without examining what happens after the ball is hit. Let's take a look at the fine art of baserunning. In our opinion, coaches on our level do one of two things when talking about, teaching, or drilling baserunning. They either spend too much time on it or they don't spend any time on it at all. As with most of what you have read in this book, we take the middle road—we believe that you must spend time talking about it and teaching it, but you can't dwell on it. Kids need to run those bases without restrictions put upon them.

Here are our rules for teaching and practicing baserunning:

1. You ready for this one? **WATCH THE BALL.** That's right. We don't believe you should be telling your kids to watch the coach and not follow the ball. They are going to watch it anyway and only they can tell when they should run, except for the turn at third. In the major leagues, most players run the bases on their own. Your kids should

also. We are not saying that you should tell them to follow the ball. This takes time and will cause players on this level to run right by the bases and in some cases miss them. We think you should teach them to "peek" at it. Find it and then run like the dickens to the next base or stay put. You should be telling your players that if they hit the ball in the alley in right center, **FIND IT** and determine whether they can go for two. The play at the plate, though, is the third-base coach's job to determine.

2. Wherever the head and hands go, the body will go. Teach lateral movement by teaching your players to stay low and throw their hands and heads in the direction they want to go. You and your players will be surprised at how much quicker they can get to the next base. Teach lateral movement in stationary drills. Have your players line up along the baseline and throw their heads and hands toward the next base, without moving. After this is mastered, put the two together.

3. Teach turning the bases the correct way. Did you ever watch TV and see a major leaguer go for "two"? You'll see that he rounds the base before heading for second. It is faster and gets the body into a straighter line toward the next base.

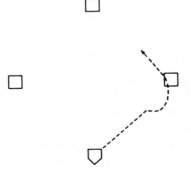

How do you teach it? Put an obstacle in the way and have your players start from the plate and go around it to first and continue to second.

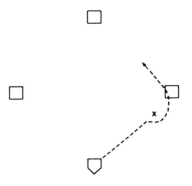

You should stress this "turning" at every base. Be careful though because your players will have a tendency to "belly" too far out. This will actually be slower. Make the "belly" just ten or twelve feet in front of the base and you will get the momentum of your players moving in the right direction.

4. Hit the inside corner of the base. Don't worry about which foot your player uses, just teach that the shortest distance between two points is a straight line and that a straight line is made by cutting the corners. Teach hitting the corner of the base.

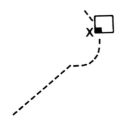

5. Finally, let them run! Teach it, drill it, practice it. Then in the games, let them run the bases! Don't get angry if a player tries to stretch a single into a double and gets thrown out. Applaud the aggressiveness. Explain why it was a bad judgment but encourage your players to be aggressive baserunners. Pete Rose did not get all those extra bases out of laziness. He *made* his hits.

SUMMARY

There is no one right or wrong way to hit, but there are certain things every good hitter must do. By combining certain batting styles and leaving the good hitters alone, you can improve the hitting of your ball club. If a player is doing something that will physically hurt him or will have to be changed later, you should change him now. The key word is control. Let the kids hit; they won't learn by taking on 3 and 0. Let them learn to run the bases. Getting from first to second or third or home increases the fun.

7

Pitching

Rock/Up
Turn
Lock
Arm Up
Follow-through

Sounds like something out of an exercise program, doesn't it? This is a list of the basic components of pitching—the five things to concentrate on.

Before we go any further, let's get one thing out in the open and over with quickly: *If you are allowing your pitchers to throw curve balls or any kind of breaking ball, you should not be coaching youth league ball.* The young arms you are working with are not ready to deal with the twisting and turning that result from throwing breaking balls; if you let them do it, you're going to ruin their arms.

However, by the time you finish reading this chapter, you won't have any need to teach curve balls; we'll show you how to get movement on the ball based purely on how it is held.

On your level of coaching baseball, the team with the best pitcher is usually the most successful. That's why most coaches put the best athlete on the mound and leave him alone as long as he throws strikes. True, your best athlete usually throws the hardest, controls his body the best, and controls what he does with the baseball the best, so you should use him and teach him, but be careful not to leave everyone else out.

Remember, your best athlete may not be there every day and some leagues allow him to pitch only three innings, so you better teach others as well. And you just may find a youngster who was made to pitch—not necessarily a good hitter or a good fielder, but oh, can he throw strikes!

The easiest way to find out who can pitch is to line up the entire club facing the fence and have them throw the ball. Watch location, watch mechanics, and watch what they do with the baseball and their arms. After this evaluation, you may find your pitchers quickly—or you may also have to watch them throwing to live batters.

MECHANICS

Since most youngsters don't throw correctly, let's start from scratch and we can *guarantee* your pitchers will improve.

THE GRIP—Refer back to Chapter 5 and see how the baseball should be held. Basically, everything on the mound is the same in terms of where the ball is held, the distance from the palm, the hand behind the ball. The only difference we suggest is that you teach your pitchers to hold the ball *between* the seams or on top of the long seams.

If your pitchers do everything else mentioned in Chapter 5, most of them will get movement on the ball by holding it off center and between the seams. The best way to test this is for you to do it yourself. Pick up the ball, throw it straight with your fingers across the seams, and then try it again with your fingers between the seams. Notice the movement of the ball! Teach that to your pitchers—it works.

THE MOTION—The main reason youth league pitchers lack good control is that they rarely throw the ball the same way twice. They rock back one time, sideways the next; they throw overhand one time, sidearm the next. Their inconsistency doesn't permit learning and can lead to frustration for both you and the player.

Your job, at least in the beginning, is to stress consistency and teach your players to get a rhythm and motion down pat. Have them use the same motion every single time they throw the ball. An easy way to teach and motivate them is to ask them to name a major league pitcher who varies his motions on each pitch. While there are a few, your players won't know them because they usually don't last long enough to develop a reputation in the big leagues.

Stress *consistency.* Help them find their motion and stick with it. What is the ideal motion? There isn't one— each pitcher will have his own way of getting the ball up there. However, there are five basic mechanical components that every good pitcher includes in his motion:

1. **Rock/Up.** The rocking motion used to initiate all movement from the mound may be the most important. The keys here are to make sure the pitcher rocks back away from the mound to start—

straight back, not to one side—and to make sure his rocking foot hits the same place behind the rubber each time.

Note that the rocking motion is joined with the hands going up and that the foot dropped is going straight back. This is the key to consistent windup—you must make sure that the step back is uniform. At the same time, teach your pitcher to bring his hands up in front of his face and behind his head. Many pitchers do not bring their hands all the way up, but if your pitcher is uniform and consistent with his rock/up movements, don't change him. If he is not, stress that he should touch the back of his neck with his hands each time he rocks; by having him make contact

with the back of his head he will have an excellent reference point for any time when he doesn't do it—he won't feel the contact. (Buzz words: **TOUCH THE NECK.**)

2. **Turn.** Now the pitcher must turn his body sideways so he can continue the throwing motion and get in position on the rubber to push. This turning of the hips and feet is very important to get his body in the throwing plane and to move his foot in front of the rubber for the push.

   Pushing, incidentally, is part of the reason why a little rabbit like Ron Guidry can throw the ball ninety miles an hour; he gets such push from the

rubber, combined with a well tuned body and consistent motion, that his arm can work with the help of his legs. Most youth league pitchers don't push, so you should be working on the push with your pitchers. One way to do that is to put your foot behind the pitcher and push back as he releases the ball. This way he will *feel* what you are talking about.

3. **The Lock.** You may want to call this part of the motion the "Drysdale/Seaver Lock." There are no two pitchers who ever did it better. To explain, the object after Rock/Up and Turn is to make sure the glove side of the body stays in *control* while the

arm has time to catch up and push forward to release the ball.

Note how the pitcher here has kept his glove side *in*, so his body is in control before he starts the push from the rubber. The best way to teach locking in is to teach your pitcher to turn his glove in and elbow out as he turns. This will force his knee, leg, and glove side to stay without losing control.

To teach the "Drysdale/Seaver Lock" to a youth league player, begin working on it without the ball and glove and without throwing. Once your pitcher learns it, he will see remarkable control improvement and will want to make it a habit.

4. **Arm Up.** You will recall that in Chapter 5 we explained that the thrower's hand is held behind and on top of the ball and *the elbow is above the shoulder.* The same thing is true for pitchers. More youth league pitchers lose control because their elbows drop than for any other reason. You must work on it over and over—without the ball and with the ball—until it becomes second nature for your pitchers to keep their elbows above their shoulders.

5. **Follow-through.** Teach your pitchers to finish their throws. All this means is that a pitcher should have his chest on his front leg and his throwing arm in the opposite pants pocket after releasing the ball. If you can teach this, you will have follow-through and more accuracy.

That's it! Just teach these simple mechanics and you will have improved accuracy. The only other thing you may want to deal with at this stage of your players'

development is when to pick up the catcher's target. Most coaches tell their pitchers to keep their eyes on the catcher's glove at all times, but there's a new theory on this—one that we subscribe to. The pitcher should take his eyes off the catcher after initiating motion and then pick him up again just before he gets ready to begin arm movement.

The theory can be tested easily. Stare at something on the wall forty to sixty feet away; now take your arms and put them above your head. If you did it right you will notice that when you stare at something too long it gets fuzzy and once you start movement with the arms it is very difficult to keep your eyes glued to the same spot. Now try it the other way. Find your spot. Stare. Look down or away and initiate arm movement and find the spot again. Notice what happens. By taking your eyes off momentarily, you now concentrate harder and the target is clearer and more easily found. If you've ever watched Fernando Valenzuela pitch you have witnessed an expert at this.

PITCHING DRILLS

There is no better way to teach pitching than by putting the catcher out there and having the pitcher throw while you stand with him. Keep the practice sessions relatively short; remember, kids' arms tire too. You won't teach much to a youngster who is tired from throwing too many pitches, and you could hurt him. Incidentally, your pitcher should not throw every day. As in weight lifting, the body needs time to rest or it will wear down. One day of throwing, with the next day off, is a good practice. To give you some idea of routine, most high school and college pitchers pitch one day, rest the second day, throw batting practice or warm-up the third, rest the fourth, and pitch again the fifth.

Think safety. When your pitcher warms up, be sure your catcher is wearing his mask and his cup. Also, be sure he has a home plate in front of him. To practice control and movement of the ball, your pitcher needs a target to throw to. Of course, your pitcher should throw the ball from the same distance each time, which means you should mark the field for the location he is throwing from.

Another useful form of pitching drill is to let your pitcher practice throwing at a target on a wall. Be sure to mark the location he is to throw from.

SOFTBALL PITCHING

Although we are dealing with both baseball and soft-ball, we have spent little time so far talking about differences in skills because there are few. The most notable difference is in pitching, and even there, care-ful analysis will show you the pitching skills we have discussed translate closely for softball as well. Let's take a look at the underhand softball throw and com-pare it with the overhand baseball throw.

The first thing to understand is that the body is better equipped to throw underhand than overhand. Surprised? Try it yourself. Feel the muscles moving both overhand and underhand. See how much more comfortable the underhand throw is? Now look at the illustrations:

Notice that the softball pitcher faces the batter as he does in baseball; has a rocking motion as he does in baseball; and pushes off the rubber after initiating movement toward home plate as he does in baseball. However, softball rules also dictate some differences. You should check the rules of your league to determine whether official adult softball rules are used or whether there are some league variations. For instance, the pitcher is often required to start with both feet on the rubber. This means some leagues will not allow him to rock back off the rubber as suggested for baseball; if so, he can still rock with body motion, but without stepping off.

Most softball leagues also require that the pitcher present the ball to the batter.

Once the pitcher has presented and stopped for a moment at the beginning of the windup, as required in the rules, he rocks and then explodes forward as in baseball, keeping the hand and ball as close to his knee

as possible. Check the illustration again and note that the follow-through brings his throwing hand next to his opposite ear.

Teach softball pitching the same way as baseball pitching. Start close and use repetition. Break the pitching motion down into a series of moves, then work for accuracy first. Once your pitcher has mastered the motion with some accuracy from a short distance, simply move him back in increments until he has reached pitching distance. Remember, no pitcher should warm up without a home plate for a target and a catcher wearing a face mask to pitch to. And, of course, the best practice of all is to throw to a hitter.

SUMMARY

Keep it simple at this age level. Stress consistency, control, and accuracy. Do not permit your pitchers (either baseball or softball) to throw curves or breaking balls; teach them to get movement on the ball by holding it between the seams. Use the buzz words **ROCK/UP, TURN, LOCK, ELBOW UP, and FOLLOW-THROUGH.**

8

Catching—
for the Catcher

Now we come to the most important player in the game: the catcher. He controls the game, Coach. If he doesn't perform, everything else goes down the drain.

Probably your biggest problem will be to get a catcher. You will have to overcome the fear kids naturally have of standing behind someone who is waving a stick in front of his face and trying to hit this hard white thing that always seems to find its way to the catcher's chest. Remember, in Chapter 3 we noted the equipment considerations that are so important to guarantee that you start the season with a catcher. Keep reminding your "volunteer" he will be able to play almost all the time if he is the only one and he might even become a willing volunteer.

On this level, it is imperative that you convince the youngster he will not get hurt. Actually, with all the equipment on, his chances of being injured are probably less than anyone else on the field. It may help to dress your "volunteer" and hit him lightly with baseballs so he can see for himself. Of course, you'll control the situation; when the youngster finds the softly tossed ball against his face mask does not make his brains fall out it will build his confidence. The same is true with the chest protector and the shin guards.

Another safety factor to consider is that if you teach the player to catch correctly, he will be even less likely to get hurt. Teach him to stay in front of the ball and to keep his head down; teach him to keep his bare hand "soft fist" and you will reduce his chance of injury.

The bottom line is that you must work with your catcher as you work with no one else on the field, not just on his skills, but on his safety confidence. Do this well and your catcher development project is on the way to success.

POSITION

Let's begin talking about catching by talking position. Not the *name* of the position—the place he stands. Too often, coaches take for granted that catchers know where to stand in the box—how far from the plate, how far from the umpire, and so forth. However, most of your players won't know, and may believe that the further they are from the hitter, the safer they are. The truth is, the closer you can get, the less chance you have of getting a foul tip off the coconut.

Science tells us that gravity takes the baseball and drives it down toward the ground. Baseball tells us that most foul tips go fairly straight before they start down. If your catcher stays closer to the batter the trajectory of the foul-tipped ball will usually pass over his shoulders or just hit the shoulders rather than the body.

Just as important, Coach, the closer your catcher is to the batter, the better chance he gives the umpire to see a strike and the less chance the ball has to go down out of the strike zone because of our old pal, gravity. Simple, isn't it? Teach this to your catcher; and tell your little guy to watch the major league catchers on television.

FEET AND BODY—Now let's look at the feet and body. The catcher's general position is the ready position, in a

crouch. His glove-side foot goes slightly ahead of the throwing-side foot; hands and arms out with shoulders square. It is important that your catcher know the difference, however, between the sign-giving stance and the throwing or ready stance.

In the sign-giving or relaxed stance, your catcher is physically capable of catching the ball, but shouldn't. To receive the baseball, he should be in a ready position, which brings him up a little on his legs with arms extended.

It is important that you spend time with your catchers on their stance and position in the box. As with pitching, what you are looking for is to have your catcher basically in the same position on every pitch.

If your catcher is comfortable in his stance, can catch the ball, and can move from the position, for goodness' sake leave him alone. Remember the rule: if it works, don't fix it. It's also true for catching. Unless you're sure your catcher's stance will not work now or later or will harm the child, leave him alone. However, you should insist that he catch with both hands. The major league catcher who started putting one hand behind his back should be shot.

> HANDS—Teach your catcher to place the bare hand next to the glove in a soft fist position; in this position a foul ball that hits the hand causes less damage (as opposed to a hard fist position that causes knuckle crunchers). Incidentally, if your catcher wants to keep his hand behind his back, watch him catch a few and you will probably note that he moves the bare hand forward on almost every pitch anyway. Therefore, teach two hands, please.

Your catcher will get better as he learns to move. The major part of the job is being able to catch the baseball, and that is greatly aided by teaching your catchers to move to the ball. No stabs, no one-hands, no smothers; move the body to the baseball on every pitch. How do you teach it? Repetition. Put your catcher in gear and start throwing to him—high, low, to the side, in the dirt. Make him go for the ball; make him do it with both hands on every single pitch. The more repetition he gets, the better he will get. Use tennis balls or sponge balls at first if you are afraid that balls off the body will discourage your beginner.

THROWING

Let's talk about throwing. The catcher is the only player on the field who has to consistently throw to a moving target. When the catcher throws to second on a steal or to first on a bunt, the player he's throwing to is moving! Think of your other players. The outfielder throws to a baseman who is usually on the base waiting for the ball; the shortstop who fields a grounder throws to a waiting first baseman; but the catcher comes up throwing on a steal and throws to a base that doesn't have a player at it yet. What does this tell you? The catcher, more than anyone else, must throw the ball straight.

For this reason, you must spend plenty of time practicing grip with your catcher. Remember what we said earlier: to keep the ball straight, hold it evenly over the seams.

Your catchers should practice getting this grip so that eventually it becomes second nature to catch the ball and grip it correctly. They can practice it at home in front of the TV or whatever. One way to practice grip is by repeatedly reaching into a bucket of baseballs blindly and coming up with the proper grip.

To keep the throw straight, coach your catcher to keep his throwing arm as close to his head as possible. Remember, if his arm is off the throwing plane, the ball will deviate from straight flight, so teach keeping it close to his ear as he throws.

LEG MOVEMENT—The most important part of the body in the catcher's throw is not the hand or the arm, it is the leg; the leg movements make the throw. There are two ways to throw from the catcher's crouch: a) step and throw, or b) pop and turn. In step and throw, the player catches the ball, steps toward second, and throws. The pop and turn, however, calls for the catcher to catch the ball, quickly turn his feet so his body is turned, and throw with a crow hop. (See the crow hop in Chapter 10.) The second way is probably better because it gets the catcher's body moving in the direction the ball is being thrown, which increases both quickness and the velocity of the ball. In other words, it helps prevent body movement away from the target by forcing the catcher to move quickly *in the direction he wants to throw.*

The best gimmick for teaching your catcher to catch, turn, and throw is the clap turn. Here, without the ball, you want your catcher to clap his hands and turn his feet as he comes up from the crouch to throwing position.

Repeat this process quickly so the player eventually begins to feel it as second nature. Remember, you should not let your catcher stand up before he starts to move his feet. It takes too much time and causes the throw to sail.

On youth league level, if you can teach your catchers to move to the ball, catch the ball, and throw the ball straight, you will have accomplished a great deal. However, there are a couple of other things he should know and think about.

FIELDING

FIELDING BUNTS—Never pick the ball up with one hand, either gloved or bare. Be sure your catcher realizes that the ball spins when bunted; it's very difficult to pick it up with the bare hand and impossible with the glove hand. Teach the glove to hand tap—making sure to bring glove and hand together at the same time. Make contact with the glove first to stop the spinning and then push the hands together with the ball between them.

THE POP UP—This is a difficult defensive play for catchers. Fortunately, the pop up behind the plate is not too common on your level because the cage is usually close to home plate. For those who play on fields that allow for pop ups the rules are simple: find the ball, hold the mask, run to the ball on the toes, toss the mask when you get to the ball, keep the back to the infield, take your time and stay cool, catch the ball above the head with thumbs together (no basket catches at the waist). Here's a hint: if the pitch was inside, most of the time the popped up ball will go to that side (and the umpire, if trained, has been taught to go the other way), so the catcher should turn to that side.

The catcher holds the mask so he won't step on it when the ball begins to move; he runs on the balls of his feet for the same reason outfielders do, to keep the ball steady in his eye; he doesn't toss the mask until he gets there; he keeps his back to the infield because the foul ball behind him spins toward the infield, or toward him; and he catches the ball above his head rather than basket style because it is easier to judge that way.

SUMMARY

If you teach mechanics correctly, your catcher will have less chance of being hurt and will develop more confidence. Teach him to stand close to the batter with hands and arms extended. Teach a comfortable but ready stance that allows maximum movement; emphasize foot movement. Teach him to use two hands for catching or fielding.

9

Playing
the Infield

A discussion of all the ins and outs of infield play could take several chapters, but for the purposes of teaching the basics to your youth leaguers let's concentrate on catching the ground ball and throwing to the right base. All other infield play is built on these skills.

READY POSITION—Everything in the infield is generated from what can be called a **READY POSITION.** This buzz word stresses to your players that their preparation for movement insures they will move in the right direction. The ready position also sets them up for the final step—catching the ball. If you watch the different major league infielders on television, you'll notice there are several forms of ready position in use. Some very successful infielders are actually moving toward the batter as the ball is pitched; others stand slightly bent; still others crouch.

The ready position permits both quick reaction and smooth movement for most young players. The knees are slightly bent, the glove-side foot is slightly in front of the other, and the hands are off the knees and in front of the

body. In this position, the player stands on the balls of his feet, rather than on his heels.

The best way to teach this position is to line up the troops after your demonstration and watch them do it. Don't allow for sloppiness; make sure the position of the body matches the diagram and then let them all practice moving from that position quickly.

After guaranteeing that your players are ready to move, it is important for you to take the time to teach them how to do it. Look back at Chapter 5, where we discussed teaching and practicing moving forward, backward, and laterally. For infielders, the lateral movement and planting of the foot must be learned or your players will reach a certain proficiency level and progress no further. Work on lateral movement with side straddles; roll the ball to each side of the infielders and have them stop, pick up, and be ready to throw. If you stop to think about it, you'll realize that at least half the ground balls young players miss get through because the player did not get to them.

MOVE/SET/THROW—What better way to describe the action necessary to make a play in the infield? We have already talked about moving; now let's deal with setting. Players have a tendency to try to get rid of the ball quickly, which is good. Unfortunately, they are often in too much of a hurry to get set, and the throw suffers. Be sure to take time to demonstrate the difference getting set makes in the throw, and then practice it. Teach planting the off foot.

Note that the player has planted the back foot as he would if he were just having a catch. This gives stability, as well as power, to the throw. Clearly, a player who is set will be in a better position to throw correctly. Now he is ready to throw, including all the mechanics we have already discussed—stability, arm up, follow-through, etc.

THE GROUND BALL

The play your infielders need to work on the most is the ball hit on the ground. Start by talking about it. Point out to your players that major leaguers spend hours on ground ball practice and instruction. If your youngsters go to a major league game, they will note that even while the rest of the team is taking batting practice, the infielders are taking extra ground balls; and if professionals do it repetitively, how much more must we do it!

1. **Keep the ball in front of you.** We talked about movement for a good reason. Your players will have much more success with ground balls if they keep them in front of them as much as possible. Then, if they miss, they may still have a chance to stop the ball with their bodies. Also, if it is in front, they will, of course, see it better.

Remember, usually players have enough time to get in front of the ball; when they don't get in front of a grounder, it's probably because they didn't move quickly enough.

2. **It's easier to bring the glove up than down.** Once you have established a good ready position for your infielders, the next logical step is to put the glove on the ground. Remember, you've been teaching your players to break in their gloves from the fingers down; the next step from there is to put those fingers on the ground.

Once the ball is hit, an infielder is not going to move with the glove on the ground, but he is going to start with the glove there and finish with the glove down before the ball gets to him.

Constantly stressing that the glove must start on the ground and finish on the ground will pay dividends for you. Don't let up during the season, either; constantly remind your infielders to be in a good ready position with the glove down.

3. **Reach out for the ball.** Most of the ground balls that your infielders reach but miss go "through the wickets" or between the legs. This usually happens because the infielder a) has let the ball play him—he has waited for the ball to come to him instead of going to it or b) has played the ball between his legs rather than out in front of his body. Be sure to stress repeatedly that your infielders must reach out to get the ball on every grounder. Reaching out gives your infielder an additional bonus—he has more time to react to the ball if it should kick off his glove or body.

The best way to teach fielding the ground ball is our old friend, repetition. Start slowly by rolling the ball from partner to partner, without gloves; then progress to thrown balls and eventually to batted balls. One practice gimmick is putting a string line on the ground with the infielder behind it and making him reach over it to get the ball.

POSITION BY POSITION

FIRST BASE—This player has to be able to catch. Most ground balls will end up being thrown to him and the more he catches the shorter the inning will be. Remind the first baseman that he has more time than anyone else to field a grounder and still make the play at first because he is closest. You may also want to teach him to go down on one knee to catch grounders.

SECOND BASE—This player also has enough time to go down on one knee to field some ground balls. Because most of the second baseman's throws are short ones, the infielder with the weakest throwing arm can play here.

SHORTSTOP—Look for a leader with sure hands to play shortstop. He has the most ground to cover and will need the best arm and the best range; he will probably be your second-best athlete.

THIRD BASE—He must have the best reaction time and be willing to have the ball hit hardest to him. He will need a good arm and should understand that he, too, has plenty of time to get the ball over to second or first.

SUMMARY

Teach fielding ground balls by stressing ready position, getting set to throw the ball, and throwing accurately. Think more about whether your infielders can catch the ball than about what each specific position does.

10

Playing
the Outfield

The last line of defense is the outfield. On this level, unfortunately, most of the batted balls end up there, yet because coaches usually take for granted that their players can catch, they often haven't practiced enough to prevent each ball to the outfield from becoming an adventure. A second problem is that we coaches often decide incorrectly where our best and worst outfielders should play. Where do you usually put your worst fielder? Why, right field, of course. But where are most of the balls hit when you have your best pitcher on the mound? Right field!

Think about it. When your best pitcher is on the mound, he usually throws faster than the hitters can react. They don't get around on the pitch and, therefore, shank the ball, which sends it to the right side of the diamond—right field.

Let's explore the skills needed to succeed in the outfield. Obviously, the thing that must be worked on the most and practiced the most on youth league level is not the fly ball, but the grounder, because most of the balls that get to the outfield either bounce through the infield or drop in front of the young outfielder. Refer back to Chapter 9 for a complete discussion of the proper way to field a ground ball, and add only one thing. Teach all of your outfielders to go down on one knee to field it. They usually have plenty of time—and if the ball gets by the outfield you are in trouble. Couple this with the understanding that most of the time on this level, your outfielder will not have to throw to make a play. Therefore, teach your players to opt for the safe side, get down on one knee, and make sure the ball does not get through. The illustration shows the proper position; remember, hands out in front!

When teaching this procedure, remember the beginning method used throughout this book: start close

together and start slowly. Line up your players without their gloves and roll the ball to them. Stress reaching out and getting down on that knee quickly. You'll have to remind them of the importance of getting up quickly as well, or they may take too much time returning the ball to the infield.

Progress to using the glove and move further away as you continue to toss the ball. From here, the natural progression is to hit fungoes. You'll find it quite easy to accustom your outfielders to fielding grounders on one knee. In fact, you may have more of a problem teaching youngsters who play both outfield and infield when to use the knee and when not to.

Catching fly balls is not really something that can be taught. Certainly, you can stress thumbs and pinkies (see Chapter 5) and you can talk about when to go back and when to come in, but the only way your players will become proficient is practice, practice, practice. There is no substitute for good old repetition.

Start slowly with the ball tossed by the coach so the players must reach up for it. Throw to one side and then to the other. Then follow the usual progression: back them up and toss the ball further and eventually move on to batted balls. Remember to hit the fly balls to the left and right sides, not just directly to the outfielders. Use batting practice as fielding practice. The fungoed ball is real, but not as real as a pitched ball off the bat.

The third skill to teach is the throw. Outfielders have both an advantage and a disadvantage when throwing. The advantage is that they have a much wider area to throw to—the ball thrown toward a player in the infield is usually sufficient; the disadvantage is that they have to throw the ball further.

Unfortunately, most outfielders tend to throw the ball higher to make sure it will reach the infield. True, it does go further but, unfortunately, the higher the throw, the longer it takes to come down and the longer it takes for the infielder to receive it.

The easiest way to emphasize this to your players is to put a runner on first base, hand the ball to an outfielder, and have him throw in to second with the man running. When he throws the "rainbow" ball, he will see the runner has a much better chance of beating the throw than when he throws on a line, even if the ball bounces. Spend time with all your players talking about why the ball thrown on a line is much better than the "rainbow." With your outfielders, especially, stress that the way they throw the ball can make the difference between an out and a run.

THE CROW HOP—Good outfielders are rarely standing still when they catch a fly ball. They are behind the ball and moving toward the infield at the catch so the momentum will help them get more strength in the throw. Even on youth league level, you can begin to teach this. If you watch your players having a catch, you will notice that many of them already hop on the throwing-side leg when they throw; they know they get more on the ball when they *hop toward the receiver*, so they do it. Your job with your outfielders is to teach this and institutionalize it.

Start teaching the crow hop without a ball. Let your outfielders take three steps foward starting on the throwing-side foot and finishing by hopping on that same foot. Once your players can do it on a run, have them add a half turn on the hop and throw an imaginary ball. Repeat until they have the movement down, then start tossing the ball to your outfielders, let them field it and start their crow hop. Make sure they get the feel of catching the ball and starting the crow hop at the same time.

Please note that the three step is used only in the outfield. When your infielders or your catcher crow hop, they should do it with only one step.

Now, how do you teach your outfielders *where* to throw the ball? As a general rule, teach them that the right fielder throws to the second baseman, the center fielder throws to second base, and the left fielder throws to the shortstop. True, this theory of relays doesn't come out of the Branch Rickey School of Baseball with its elaborate cutoff system; but then, Branch Rickey didn't coach the Fourth Grade Bombers. You have to decide how sophisticated your team is before you decide to teach a cutoff system. If you start them with this system, you'll find your team will get the ball back in to where the action is better than the other teams in most youth leagues.

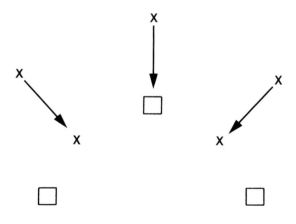

The other strategy you'll want to teach your outfielders is the back-up. Teach these rules:

1. Everybody backs up the infield on *every* ball hit to the infield.
2. Every outfielder backs up the other outfielders.
3. Unless they are fielding the ball or there are men on base, the catcher and the right fielder back up the first baseman when the ball is thrown to first base from the infield.

POSITION BY POSITION

The Right Fielder should have the best arm because he has to throw the furthest.

The Center Fielder should be the one who catches best because he will get the ball most often and will be the first back-up for both of the others.

The Left Fielder can be the poorest defensive player of the three.

SUMMARY

Work more on catching the ground ball than on catching the fly ball. If you have done a good job of teaching thumbs and pinkies, teaching how to catch the fly ball should be easy. Stress throwing on a line from the start. Teach the crow hop and the simplest cutoff system. The best way to drill outfield skills is by repetition.

11

Managing and Coaching a Game

Buzz words—concentration—crowd and parent management—cooperating with officials, opposing managers, and your assistant coaches—these are some of the leadership factors involved in letting each child play the best he or she can. Your modeling will last a lifetime.

RULES OF THE GAME

Your league will give you a copy of the rules and regulations. Study them carefully. Your team will want you to stand up for their rights if another coach challenges a ruling or procedure. You and your team will also feel more confident if you "know the ropes." If a rule isn't clear to you, get it clarified immediately. You won't want to waste practice time teaching bunting if bunting is not allowed.

Youth leagues often adopt their own rules. Some, for example, require that all members of the team must bat, so you may have a twelve-to-fifteen person batting order. Other regulations might include using a coach as pitcher, or requiring that each player must play the field at least half the game and never miss a turn at bat. One practice we like is to allow only two walks in an inning; after the second walk, only strikes are called. This stops the children from walking the bases and the game is played to develop the skills of hitting, catching, running, throwing, and thinking baseball.

GAME STRATEGY

We could discuss strategy for hours and not begin to scratch the surface. Major leaguers will tell you that in ten or twenty years they never saw the same game twice. In children's games, multiply that by ten. Every hit can be an adventure; every pitch a surprise.

The key to teaching strategy is to keep reminding yourself of the ages of your players. Many children are just beginning to anticipate and think ahead. When they throw the ball to the wrong base, remind yourself that they may not make that mistake next year. Coaches who scream and shout over every lapse are only creating increased difficulties.

Just short of your total frustration point, you will somehow have to find the strength to repeat your directions again. Have faith; many aspects of the game will somehow, sometime "jell" in the children's minds and there will be that great day when you will witness the beautiful event. In the meantime, be descriptive and patient. Continue trying to find different ways to demonstrate the concept.

SOME BASIC CONSIDERATIONS

Giving your players an opportunity to play different positions at practice and in games is very important to their understanding of the requirements and possibilities of each position. Ideally, every child should try every position during the course of the season. As he or she plays more, more conceptions will form.

Putting a child who has always been an outfielder at third base allows him to get a feel for the player who has been letting a few get by or has underthrown to first on occasion. As you explain the new position, demonstrate the correct techniques. At third, for example, bend over, feint a cradling of the ball, and pantomime a throw to first. Remember, you are always demonstrating the correct throwing techniques you have taught the entire team in throwing and catching practice. Be constantly aware of your modeling; children do what you *do*, not what you *say.*

Teach geography—every position has its own turf. Use a diagram of the field to let each player know his responsibility. As your best athlete, your pitcher will probably be your best fielder, so he should be allowed to field almost anything he can reach. Teach backing up on ground balls and on the throw to a base.

Spend some time teaching your players what to do when runners are on base. Have drills where you hit grounders to each infield position with different bases occupied. Ask each player where he will throw the ball if he gets it. If they don't understand a force play at second, act the play out and then practice it. The faster they learn to react to situations, the better they'll look and the more successful they'll be.

Meet with your assistants at the start of the season and agree on what the first and third base coaches should do. Be sure they understand that children in the younger grades may have to be urged to run by the base instead of sliding or holding up as they run toward it. Teach them well and hope they show up for the games.

GAME BEHAVIOR

Cheering, being supportive, praising, and sharing an accomplishment with a child are obviously excellent modes of behavior for you, your assistants, and the relatives and friends who come to a game or practice. Don't be afraid to share some of the suggestions in Chapter 1 with the spectators.

You can ask the parents to come to the first practice and talk to them as a group, expressing to them how you feel about comments directed to you and the players during the game. Communicate to them what your approach will be and suggest some guidelines. Some will be participating for the first time and will appreciate knowing how they can cooperate with you. The experienced parents will be projecting feelings they have had about past coaches. You want to inherit all their good thoughts and none of the bad. You can reinforce this meeting in a follow-up information sheet to be sent home later.

CROWD AND FANS

What would a game be without fans? Well, sometimes it may seem like a good idea. You know the times we mean. Ninety-five percent of the fans are sober, gentle people who know they are watching children, not professionals. However, there may be times—and you might as well prepare yourself—when the other 5 percent will get out of hand.

Begin by reinforcing the behavior of the 95 percent in the stands. Keep your own calmness intact by staying to the business at hand as long as possible and protecting your children. If the situation gets completely intolerable, confer with the officials. Refer to the league rules about crowd behavior. The officials may decide to remind the crowd that a forfeit could occur. But do everything you can to avoid that moment. Your best defense is your offense; your own relationship with your team's parents and neighbors and your behavior are at the heart of your diplomatic strategy.

OFFICIALS

Begin each game with a chat with the opposing coach and the officials, reviewing the most pertinent rules. It isn't at all uncommon to have an official lapse into high school regulations and surprise you with a "new" ruling during a game. Gaining the officials' concentration at the beginning can avoid mistakes and bad examples during the game. If you have worked with the officials and other coaches previously, you know what to expect and can change your pregame conference accordingly. Remember, the official, too, is trying his best. He's not a major league umpire either, and he may make mistakes. Consider them just that—mistakes. Remember also, the way you behave toward an official sets an example for your players.

RECORD KEEPING

You'll need a written lineup and a sheet to keep score. More extensive records are generally unnecessary and may do more harm than good. "Most valuable player" awards detract from the team effort you are building. Noticing individual improvement and allowing each team member to appreciate his own and his teammates' efforts when they try their best are much more important in building team spirit than keeping track of who has the most hits, strikeouts, errors, and so forth.

KEEPING SCORE

Use a modified version of a major league score sheet to keep track of the progress of the game. List the batting order and position each player is fielding down the left side, leaving a space between names if your league does not bat around and you have to substitute players. Make a row of squares across the page for each player to represent the innings. Each time a player bats, his square for that inning will show his progress around the bases. One, two, three, or four lines across the center of the box indicates a single, double, triple, or home run; a blackened triangle at the corner of the box shows which base he reached, using the lower right hand corner as first and the lower left as home. An "O" in the center of the box shows an out, a "K" is a strikeout, "BB" is a base on balls, and "e" is an error. At the end of each inning, simply add up the marks in the lower left hand corners and record total runs at the bottom of the column for the inning.

	1	2	3	4	5	6
Jack Armster, ss	K					
Betty Martin, lf	◄—					
Billy Green, 1b	O					
Joe White, c	◄≡					
Larry Fox, 3b	O					
Mary Todd, p						
Hits/Runs	2/1	/	/	/	/	/

Jack struck out; Betty hit a single; Billy made an out; Joe hit a triple, scoring Betty; Larry made the third out; Mary will be the first player at bat in the second inning.

For Your Clipboard

Every good coach realizes he can't remember every-thing, so he makes notes and brings them to practice. (Now you know why coaches always have clipboards!) Try using these "buzz words" to trigger memory and aid teaching.

THROWING THE BALL	YOUR NOTES

The buzz words:
  Grip
  Hand Behind the Ball
  Arm Elevation
  Shoulder Rotation
  Stride
  Crow Hop
  Follow-through

CATCHING THE BALL	YOUR NOTES

The buzz words:
  Move
  Two Hands
  Thumbs and Pinkies
  Arm Extension
  Bend
  Cradle

EXTENDING THE THROW AND THE CATCH . . . FIELDING

THE GROUND BALL	YOUR NOTES

The buzz words:
   Ready Position
   Knees Bent
   Balls of Feet
   Get to It First
   Reach Out
   Be a Backup

THE FLY BALL	YOUR NOTES

The buzz words:
   Find Ball
   Run First
   Thumbs and Pinkies
   Be a Backup

NEW BUZZ WORDS	YOUR NOTES

The single most difficult skill in baseball is hitting a round ball with a round bat. True, some good hitters are born . . . but others can be made if taught correctly.

HITTING	YOUR NOTES
The buzz words:	
Stance	
Head and Eyes	
Grip	
Elbow Position	
Arm Position	
Initiating Movement	
Weight Back	
Hip Rotation	
Where to Contact Ball	
Follow-through	

NEW BUZZ WORDS	YOUR NOTES

PITCHING   YOUR NOTES

The buzz words:
    Hands/Grip
    Feet
    Rock/Up
    Touch the Neck
    Turn
    Push Off the Rubber
    Drysdale/Seaver Lock
    Elbow Up
    Arm Up
    Follow-through

CATCHING   YOUR NOTES

The buzz words:
    Position
    Feet
    Body
    Stance
    Soft Fist
    Two Hands
    Grip
    Foot Movement

DRILLS AND GIMMICKS

The buzz words:
  "21"
  No Gloves
  Short Toss
  Fungo
  Running Bases
  Pickups
  Knees Down
  One Leg Up
  Touch the Ground
  Quick Movement Drill
  Clap Turn
  Bucket of Balls
  Throw to Wall Target
  String a Line
  Wooden Paddle
  The Batting "T"
  Rubber Hose
  Sponge Ball
  Whiffle Ball

YOUR POSITION-BY-POSITION REVIEW

CATCHER

PITCHER

FIRST BASE

INFIELD

OUTFIELD